RUSH LIBRARY

ANNE STREET PRESS

Æ

ASSOCIATED EDITIONS

Commissioned in 2006 and completed in 2009, Rush Library came to pass through the combined efforts of many people – whose common purpose helped to achieve it – Fingal County Council, the design team, and the intelligent and skilful work of the contractors Dunwoody and Dobson and their sub-contractors. Particular thanks are due to the Fingal County Manager David O Connor, to the County Architect Marguerite Murphy, Senior Architect Fionnuala May and Senior Quantity Surveyor Sean Sloyan, to Jack Tritschler In Boyd Creed Sweett Quantity Surveyors, James Fegan and Ciaran Kennedy in Barrett Mahony Structural Engineers, Frank O Callaghan, Susan Jones and Michael McLoughlin in McArdle McSweeney Services Engineers and Leona Roche in McCullough Mulvin Architects , to Paul Duffy and Dan Bolger in Dunwoody and Dobson and to Paul Harris, Rina Mullett, Phyllis Carter, Senan Turnbull, Angela Hayes, Geraldine Bollard and Yvonne Reilly in Fingal County Council Libraries Division.

McCullough Mulvin Architects is an architecture and urban design practice; much of their work has been in the design of cultural and civic projects around Ireland. The practice pursues modern architecture for very particular contexts, a particular resonance in schemes combining new interventions into old buildings The work is extended through publication *(A Lost Tradition, Palimpsest, Dublin: An Urban History)*, teaching and research. An investigation of common ground between modern architecture and the idea of place is at the heart of the office's pursuit; this book on Rush Library – exploring architectural layering and the survival of memory in the context of change – is intended as the first of a series of publications contributing to a wider debate about the course of architecture in Ireland.

McCullough Mulvin Architects
1 Setanta Place, Dublin 2, Ireland
Tel 01 707 9555
Mail: Info@mcculloughmulvin.com
Web: mcculloughmulvin.com

This book is published by Associated Editions and Anne Street Press

ISBN 978-1-906429-10-2

Distributed by Associated Editions

Associated Editions
33 Melrose Avenue, Dublin 3, Ireland
www.associatededitions.ie

Anne Street Press
2 Leeson Park, Dublin 6

Text © 2010 Niall McCullough and Raymond Ryan

Photographs © 2010 as listed in the captions. Where no attribution is made, photographs are by McCullough Mulvin Architects

Design & layout: Kevin Dunne, Vermillion Design
Art Direction: Anne Brady, Vermillion Design

Image Opposite: New external sign in manufacture. Photo Dunwoody and Dobson

This book is part funded by

Fingal County Council
Comhairle Contae Fhine Gall

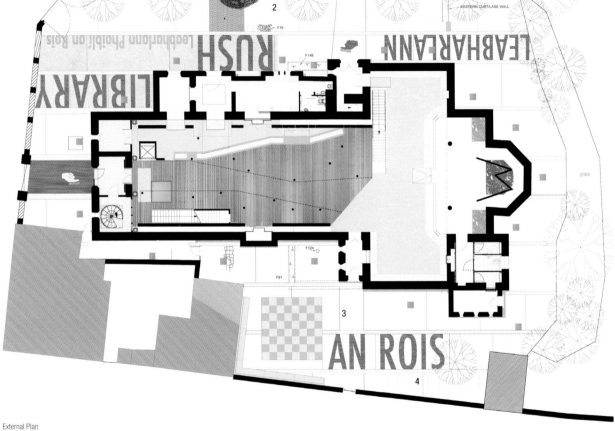

External Plan

1 Perimeter wall
2 18th century churchyard paving
3 Chessboard
4 Indented names

TIME AND CHANGE

Modern architecture is founded on the idea of the new – new functions in new buildings for a renewed world; there is a fertile gap between this optimistic outlook and the interventive reality of construction – form displacing space, scouring out the earth, altering contexts, feeding off the existing world as it transforms it. This is clearly on a scale; at its most extreme, change invades existing architecture; older buildings encapsulate a specific history – and that requires a commentary. History is another language – at once familiar and treacherous; it cannot be treated as a linear preparation for current existence; there is always a gap between its interpretation and the reality, continual surprise that ends with a questioning of ones own prejudice. It is, of necessity, an enigma, balanced between what it reveals and what it can never reveal – laden with distortion and misremembering; altering functions, making interventions to historic buildings thus requires careful navigation. At another level, re-use represents a straightforward recycling of materials and spaces, but it also begs an understanding of the ideas within the original building – sustainability of meaning as well as fabric – layered under and woven through modern form. This synthesis – old against new – is like music; it is appropriate to the multivalent character of 21st century thought – and the fractured nature of modern existence. In an age of regulation and over-management, the awkward fact of old things endures; approximate shapes – and changes to them – cannot be reduced to rules and offer embedded resistance to the worst aspects of globalisation – specific, about a place, never generic, certainly unique, occasionally original. This radical change within a strong context is central to the Irish and European architectural tradition, though seldom highlighted as such. As an approach to modern architecture, it is under constant threat from the shadow of extremes – from conservationists who want simple truths or from designers who equate modernity with 'newness – and simply don't understand it. This is the fate of all art between safe zones; it is a freedom of thought and expression that should be vigorously defended. The book is about the potential of such work explored through a single project – Rush Library. Libraries in Ireland have provided quiet public space for well over a century, fuelling the passion for books, reading and literature that is at the heart of a learning and thinking culture. The new library in Rush continues this tradition; this book is about the building – how a working library was made out of an old church, a modern intervention inserted into the existing fabric to support a new use.

Following pages: The landscape of North County Dublin.

RUSH RE-PRESENTED

Raymund Ryan

Curator, The Heinz Architectural Center
Carnegie Museum of Art, Pittsburgh

In the twentieth century, progress was often believed to be somehow independent of the past, to be manifest in brave new phenomena or artefacts free from history. Nowadays, for ecological as much as cultural reasons, history has regained a certain power. History as politics, history as temporality, history as narrative. One of the curious characteristics of the Celtic Tiger era was our seeming collective belief in global universalisation. Now in more straightened times, there is an opportunity to reconsider context and resources, heritage and an optimal pace for daily life. This I believe is the future presented and reinforced by McCullough Mulvin's conversion of a deconsecrated Victorian church, St. Maur's, to a lively modern library for the people of Rush.

Niall McCullough and Valerie Mulvin's career has evolved from their understanding of history, both ancient and modern, to an ability to incorporate not only physical fragments but the grain of the past into new construction projects. Their early book, or illustrated taxonomy, *A Lost Tradition: The Nature of Architecture in Ireland* (1987) revealed a literacy in Irish building types – grand and modest, institutional and vernacular – that has matured into an appreciation for the layers of intervention found in many Irish buildings and, without doubt, in most Irish towns. This eye for historical nuance and for the true story of construction has informed their design of galleries in Dublin and Sligo and of libraries in Tubbercurry, Waterford and, now, Rush.

The church is but one linear element in an unusually linear town plan. The rows of houses and attenuated street leading to the harbour find a contemporary echo in the striation of paving, planting and supergraphics that McCullough and Mulvin use to re-order a rather bleak churchyard. The church faced of course to points east and to the sun's daily ascension above the Irish Sea. Today a new bipartite door, punctured by circles, inhabits the original doorway and leads on axis to an apse still animated by stained glass windows. Flanking both longitudinal walls and propped on skinny steel columns are two long and irregular balconies, one open with balustrade, the other wrapped in walnut to enclose a communal meeting room.

St. Maur's remains largely intact. Influenced perhaps by the maritime context, the architects' primary intervention is not unlike a ship-in-a-bottle. Their new structures slide into place separated from the Victorian walls by glazed floor strips and expanding into the ecclesiastical void without touching the ceiling above. McCullough and Mulvin tactically position slots or windows to visually connect up into roof trusses and down onto remnants of an earlier church. One might think of these moves as non-invasive superimpositions and, conversely, as operations to peel away the unnecessary in order to frame views, light and "found" architectural elements. Thus Rush Library allows the old and the new, local memories and future learning, to co-exist.

View from behind main desk. Photo Ros Kavanagh.

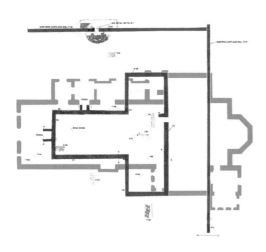

Above: Plan of 18th century chapel under existing church. Drawing M Gowen and Co.

Top right: Interior before commencement of the work

Bottom right: Exterior before commencement of the work

Intervention within the nave of the church. Photo Ros Kavanagh

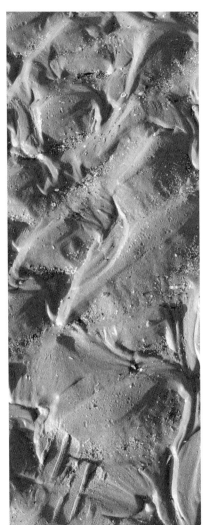

Context: The Land, The Shore, The Sea

View of Lambay Island from the Tower

RADICAL CONTEXT

Niall McCullough

This book is about a church that became a library in a small town in North Co. Dublin – a radical conservation project using place and fabric to support a new architecture. Designing a library is always challenging; making a library in a disused church by the sea even more so, and there are many threads to untangle in reaching a satisfactory resolution. Architecture is all about ideas – and so questions can be asked which then influence the design – in this case questions about how libraries should work in the 21st century, what an appropriate 21st century public space might be like, how the idea of 'place' can be harnessed in a clear-sighted, unsentimental way? How can architects develop an open-ended way of thinking about old buildings, prepared to be bold in designing interventions, defusing history, forging a meaningful synthesis between new and old?

Thinking about architecture is always a mixture of the personal and the objective. Our access to libraries was through books; interest in books is personal; books are sensual, disparate, infinitely varied objects; ordering them on your own shelves is a delicious pleasure. Reading remains, for many people, a quiet, hot, passion; how to make space that sustains it should be a key concern for architects. The idea of the great Library at Alexandria was an impossible but beautiful dream, to place the summation of human knowledge in one location, not least to make an attempt at immortality; that grand plan is, by its nature, undercut by the anarchic diversity of information books contain – a vivid representation of the frail brilliance of human endeavour. And, although a library might still aspire to that concept of universal diversity through books or digital media, it is clear that they cannot simply be storehouses and must create discrete spaces for both dreaming and thinking; increasingly – and this is especially true of buildings in wet climates like Ireland – they have a role as interior public spaces, theatres of life for performance and observation.

The entangled history, materials, traditions, smell, light, vistas of a physical location are experienced by many people; responses are best described as stories – funny or sad – which can be told in an infinite number of ways. When consideration of place arose in the context of Rush, very specific things came to mind – the disciplined vegetable drills around the town, wind, the need for shelter, the relationship with the sea. North County Dublin has a particular character where the plains of Fingal unfold along the Irish Sea in a series of intimate bays; the Romans made their only foray into Ireland along this coast. Rush is surrounded by a gridded landscape overlaid by a suburban sprawl which owes its particular form to the field network beneath it. You can still step onto the earth to pick up a cabbage; there are sandy paths between greenhouses to the sea. Lambay Island is visible between the houses, mythical, like an island in a Tintin book, mute, unattainable.

St. Jerome in his study

That process starts a train of thought about islands, being on one, looking at another, about Ireland, which has always been at the edge of Europe, about the traditional image of the scholar as an island in a busy world. It highlights the sea and the coastline; coasts have reefs which need to be lit from the land; when closely examined, they are indented and extremely long – like a very involved storey in a book. A library by the sea should have this poetic consciousness – its architecture responsive to the boundlessness of the water, to the lightness of boats, to its position on the boundaries of land and sea, to isolation and contemplation.

Responding to geographical place is not the same as making interventions into old buildings, where the response is more condensed, conditioned by specific historic choices. This kind of work requires a formal reply to the old fabric, a dance of culturally – laden, a-nostalgic alternatives to the original form and memory. Does the project use existing geometries, cancel them, play a game with them – use inexpensive or colourful materials? Responses work at any scale; they can be made through ten tiny things or one big one, registers on a scale rather than differences in kind; it is a good example of working with ordinary things to make something extraordinary. Ireland, for all its violent history of destruction and reconstruction, is full of such buildings, churches extended piecemeal over time, towns evolving into cities – forms which appear picturesque to modern eyes but are utterly rational – and usually radical – in the context of their own time. Adding to them offers participation in an evolutionary process: this is only one more layer; there will be more, like barnacles accumulating on the hull of a boat – a distance from modern obsessions with a finished, polished, by implication immutable, product.

It is hard to re-establish the balance of this work for the present day, harder again to propose radical change to historic structures which runs with their meaning, adding a layer to ones already laid down. Decisions on what should be done are subject to judgement – they can only be decided on a building by building basis. Some structures should simply be conserved, others are open for change; many historic buildings in Ireland – simple but culturally laden – seem suited to such work. This approach has formed a significant part of our work in projects such as the Model Arts and Niland Gallery, Sligo Courthouse or in Waterford City Library. Here, new elements alter circulation routes and complete geometries incipient in the original plan; the buildings have an embedded belief in urbanity, a density expressed in the contrast of forms, materials and the manipulation of light.

Churches in Ireland are commonly of the 19th century and carry with them the emotional baggage of an oppressive past – some real, some imaginary – a particular local sensitivity that links brute monumentality of form and hardness of finishes to a perceived inflexibility of religious expression. St.Maur's fell into that camp; the church dominates the village green on the western edge of Rush, its grey stone walls

Model Arts and Niland Gallery, Sligo. Photo Christian Richters

enclosing a gloomy cruciform of pinks, white marble, and machined Victorian glass – a prosaic container of space, ready for change. There is a focus of intensity in any project; in Rush, this happened inside; the exterior retained its status as a generic urban monument in the town. Clearly a public building, it has to be explored to be fully understood; there are no easily consumable images of change, only small clues to its altered state.

The design generated a dialogue between the muted – but intense – religious origins of the church and library requirements for bookshelves, seating, and an art space. The plan built up a layered response, first by respecting and conserving the existing fabric, secondly by harnessing the 'sense' of the existing architecture, thirdly by making an intervention that turned the key on this sketched-in setting, forming spaces that allowed a library to function, to be completed by books, furniture and people. This approach adjusts or overlays the existing elements rather than obliterates them; old and new gain by proximity – a matter of tone and light falling on surfaces as much as heavy rooms and structures.

The roof was repaired using natural slates, the Gothick ceiling carefully cleaned down, the monuments pieced together, windows re-leaded, the typical wood-grained doors and lobbies conserved, the value of ordinary, even humdrum, elements of religious life taken as valuable in themselves – an absence of excluding judgement. The interior was painted white on a lime plaster base, luminous, a ghost of itself; sections left off to expose the underlying material. One arbitrary hole was cut into the ceiling to reveal the roof structure. Existing buildings always play a double game; the decision to make an intervention – and dig foundations – itself revealed an archaeology of walls belonging to the earlier 18th century chapel – change trumped by a hidden weave in the fabric. The walls were incorporated into the project, visible through glass in the floor near the entrance.

The essential geography of the existing building – the cruciform plan, highly symbolic ideogram of crucifixion and the way of the cross – was re-utilised as an armature for the new. The West door remained as the library entrance; the chancel, stripped to its brickwork core, made a found space for art at the natural focus of the building; secondary functions were located in a network of side chapels and sacristies. The intervention was constructed as a walnut plane filling the nave, running across the floor and up on both sides, its tense gravity like a folded page from a book or a paper aeroplane. When flattened out, it appears like a suit of clothes or a cut-out from a cereal packet; pulled taut, it has a kind of unreliable stability, an inverted U – with two galleries, one narrow, the other – wider – supporting an enclosed lecture and performance space. Gothic architecture is intensely felt; Victorian Gothick a sketched-in version which mimics its structural tension and emotional intensity; something of the folded shape has a Gothic edge in its sharp angular balance.

Waterford City Library. Photo Christian Richters

The genealogy of the new echoes the form of galleries found in such churches. Like St Jerome in his room, it is a warm shell inside the existing carcass, form simultaneously containing and excluding space; like the Laurentian Library, it is barely contained, pushing tensely against the existing walls. It makes its own world, a seaweed-like desk floating away from the entrance. In three dimensions, the central route becomes a city street, its shape deforming the route, forcing it to meander, glimpses of a coloured termination lost and found again, a screen in the art space repeating the geometry on a smaller scale. There are judgements on proportion and extent. The wooden enclosure re-shapes the section, a judgement on the degree of space held and space left floating free above and around it. On plan, it comes just to the edge of the nave, defining an interstitial zone – the crossing space – as a field of play between the elements. Accepting the principles of clarity and reversibility, the new stands distinct from the old, creating impossibly thin vertical spaces against the outer walls; where gallery railings were cut, they were cut cleanly through.

In the massive volumes of traditional buildings with their lost spaces, where the interiors always seem to hang from the rafters like a stage-set, the intervention seems like a light papery thing – tentative, a Russian doll-like interior world within an interior world. Yet it displaces space; it stands all around the nave and yet in it: passing through its columns is like walking through a forest. The spaces within, and the views beyond change in combination as perspectives alter. Both entwine around light; inserting a form into an older one refracts the light, bends it in line with the new across the old framework. In Ireland, light moves all the time, does not conform to the Mediterranean model of a single moving shaft like a sundial; sunlight glints, is covered, dark, then light; the interplay of architecture with this phenomenon is truly local.

There is a sensual play here; the intervention lends weight to existing elements dramatically revealed; the old lobby which remained as the library entrance, the confessional box turned into a music listening booth, an assessment on the affinity between forms, how accommodating one can be to the other without loss of integrity. This extends to materiality – there is a strong contrast between the old vault and the new walls which is, in some ways, the reverse of expectation – one reflective yet heavy, the other lightweight, but also light absorptive. Planning the project brought opportunities. Environmental aspects were closely studied; the intervention changes the acoustics of the building and provides a network of heating pipes and panels – it acts like a giant radiator. Sustainable choices were made to minimise the impact on the material quality of the existing fabric. The extensive ceiling void was filled with plant and insulation; the ground plan was renewed as an 'intelligent floor' of services, heating and cables, but the external walls were left alone.

Functionally, the intervention creates identifiable – but penetrable – niche space for individual functions. The adult library and desk are near the entrance; children roam the transepts; local studies occupy the galleries with the enclosed lecture and meeting room. The furniture extends the enclosure. Bookshelves become part of the architecture; people sitting, talking, browsing, complete it and bring it alive, decoupling it from antiquity to provide an integrated hierarchy of modern spaces at different scales, spaces to be lost in, rooms for individual dreaming and thinking, group areas, noisy areas, quiet areas. It also works as public space or a theatre, with areas to see and be seen from.

External change is minimal – a sign, a metal book on a gable, a new door. The only significant expression is the light box in the tower – a lantern to knowledge visible out to sea. On the ground, the churchyard became a garden with concrete strips inset with names, interspersed with drainage channels planted with grasses and vegetables, the spirit of the graveyard – and the towns agricultural basis – extended as a garden. This protected public space, it stands – without pressure – in a wider, semi-public, landscape of car parks and grass – gardens within gardens beside other garden plots and greenhouses – the space of the intervention opening out and extending down the roads to the sea.

This work is about making ordinary public buildings in small communities, but it contains the possibility of architectural expression which can be particular in small ways and make an honourable pact with the past. In the end, the project succumbs to the process of habitation – people occupy space; the work reappears through their eyes as an adventure– and already a potential ruin, its own archaeology.

Opposite: Library exterior. Photo H. Williams

Art space from the gallery. Photo H Williams

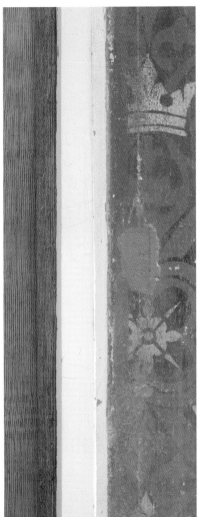

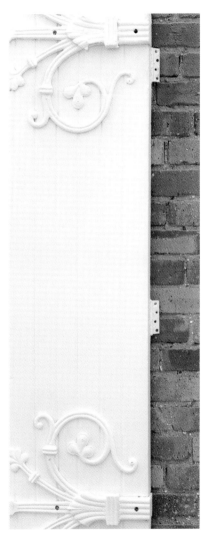

Material Conservation: chancel detail, chancel detail, door retained as wall paneling. Photo H Williams

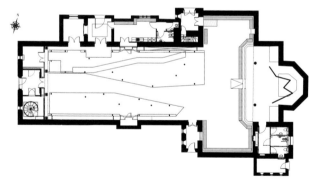

Clockwise from top left: Church interior before
intervention; St Werburgh's Church Dublin. Photo
Irish Times: Matt Kavanagh; Plan of intervention;
Laurentian Library staircase

Opposite: The Intervention: Study model

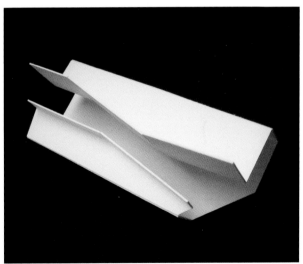

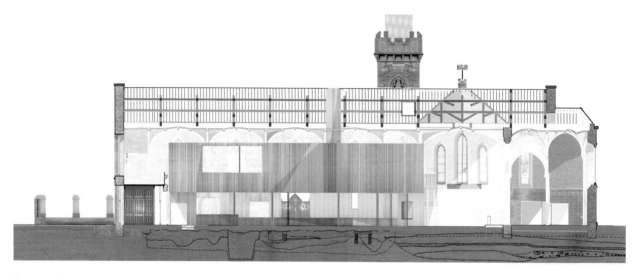

Above: Long section of library

Right: Cross section of library

Opposite top: Ground Floor Plan
1 Entrance
2 Art space
3 Main Desk
4 Adults
5 Children
6 Staff area

Opposite bottom: First Floor plan
1 Meeting and Performance Space
2 Local Studies area

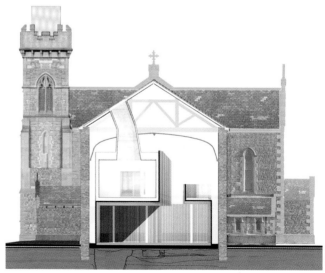

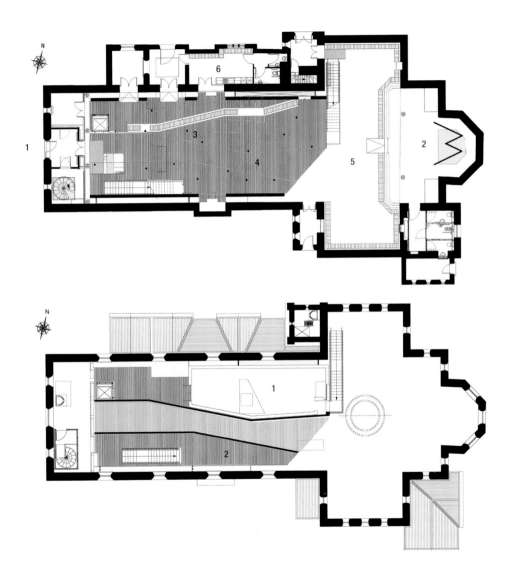

View to main entrance. Photo Ros Kavanagh

View from Main Entrance towards art space. Photo Ros Kavanagh

View towards art space. Photo Ros Kavanagh

Separation of new work from existing fabric. Photo H. Williams

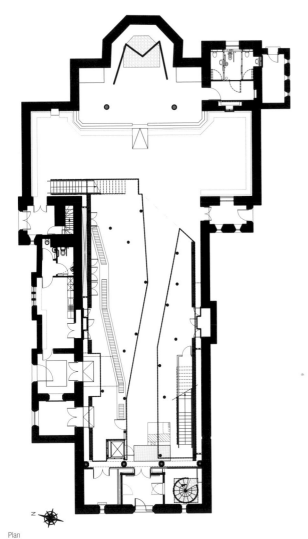

Plan

Gallery rail cut through. Photo H Williams

Nave (above); Detail with wall plaque (above right). Photos Ros Kavanagh

Opposite: View of intervention from art space. Photo Ros Kavanagh

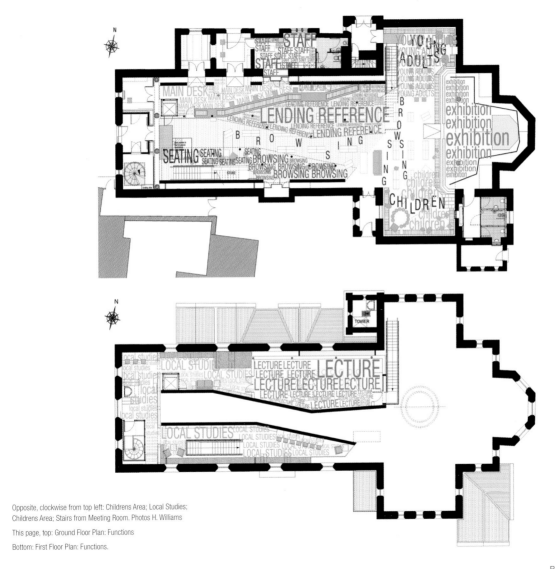

Opposite, clockwise from top left: Childrens Area; Local Studies; Childrens Area; Stairs from Meeting Room. Photos H. Williams

This page, top: Ground Floor Plan: Functions

Bottom: First Floor Plan: Functions.

The Library in Use. Photo H. Williams

The Library in Use. View from the Gallery. Photo H. Williams

External paving. Photo Ros Kavanagh

Opposite: Library garden. Photo Ros Kavanagh

Above: Library Exterior. Photo H. Williams

Right: Library in context

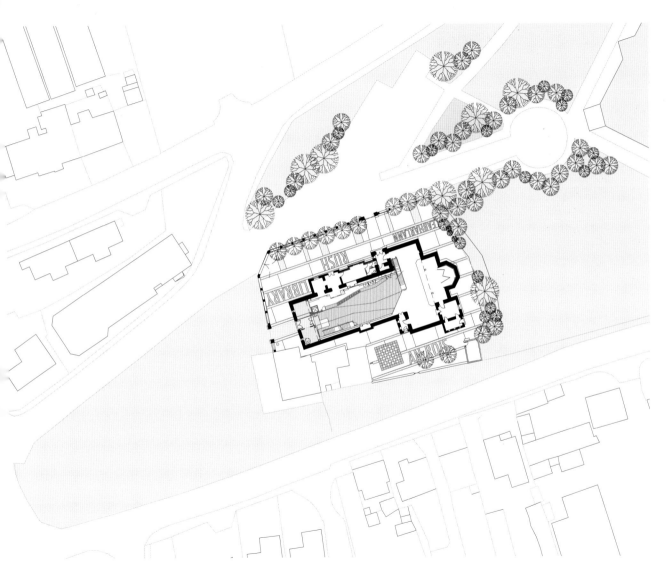